Intergenerational Tai Chi: An Anti-Ageism and Memory Improvement Activity for Children and Seniors

Featuring Randy Tai Chi and Grandpa Frank

DR. MAURICE R. OLFUS

AuthorHouse™
1663 Liberty Drive
Bloomington, IN 47403
www.authorhouse.com
Phone: 833-262-8899

Because of the dynamic nature of the Internet, any web addresses or links contained in this book may have changed
since publication and may no longer be valid. The views expressed in this work are solely those of the author and do
not necessarily reflect the views of the publisher, and the publisher hereby disclaims any responsibility for them.

Interior photos by Dr. E. Brian Ashton
Back Cover photo of Tai Chi teacher, Ms. Shigeko Carter with her student, Randy Olfus

This book is printed on acid-free paper.

ISBN: 978-1-6655-4795-6 (sc)
ISBN: 978-1-6655-4794-9 (e)

Print information available on the last page.

Published by AuthorHouse 01/12/2022

authorHOUSE®

Intergenerational Tai Chi: An Anti-Ageism and Memory Improvement Activity for Children and Seniors

Featuring Randy Tai Chi
and Grandpa Frank

Contents

Introduction

Ageism impacts the mental health of both the young and old at a calculated annual treatment cost of $63 billion, according to a Yale School of Public Health study.[1]

To minimize the cause, effects, and financial social burden associated with ageism, the World Health Organization (WHO) recommends a least costly approach.[2] Community ageism awareness and activism can be an effective intervention strategy.

In this story, Randy Tai Chi and his friends at Gratefulness Elementary School become ageism awareness activists. How will their use of intergenerational tai chi as a community activity strategy help keep the ills of ageism far, far away from the town of Gratefulness? Will it work?

---

[1] "Ageism: A Social Determinant of Health That Has Come of Age."

[2] *Campaigning to Tackle Ageism: Current Practices and Suggestions for Moving Forward.*

Acknowledgments

1. The Gray Panthers

2. Defense for Children International

3. Alzheimer's Association

4. AARP

5. World Health Global Campaign to Combat Ageism

Dedicated to the memory of Randy
Olfus' god-grandfather, Francis Joseph
Farren, Jr., aka Grandpa Frank

In memory of Randy Olfus' God-Grandfather, Francis Joseph Farren, Jr. (AKA Grandpa Frank). And to young activists that are leading the fight against age discrimination.

Chapter 1: The Need for Ageism Awareness at Town of Gratefulness Elementary School

Narrator: After briefing the mayor, the two smart scientists smartly exit Mayor Howard B. Thyname's office. That is because exiting rooms smartly is what smart people often do.

Their findings are on his desk—a book and reports, all relevant to the problem at hand.

The mayor reminds himself to breathe in and out slowly. He relaxes his shoulders, clears his mind, steadies his hands, and slowly brings a report to eye level to read. "Ageism is the underreported bias. It is culturally acquired, and almost everyone over a certain age has experienced it."

With furrowed brow, he sets the report aside with his right hand and flips through other research papers with his left.

Mayor Thyname: Hmm. Older people who have a positive self-perception about aging live seven and a half years longer than others, have better balance and less anxiety, sleep better, and have higher self-esteem and better cognition.[3] Interesting.

Narrator: As the mayor continues to read, he feels surprised.

Mayor Thyname: What's this? Positive habits and behaviors about aging are cultivated early in a child's life. That means if behaviors are changed early in children's lives, there will be no need to increase taxes to cover public medical costs when they reach retirement age. Excellent! Now, how can I use this information to help with my reelection campaign? I need

---

[3] "Longevity Increased by Positive Self-Perception."

a campaign slogan. How about "Only Mayor B. Thyname can make the town of Gratefulness stress-free, age friendly, and the best place to live"? That works. Genius!

Narrator: Full of fresh ideas, the mayor quickly places a call to Principal Ortiz of Gratefulness Elementary School.

Chapter 2: How to Make Ageism Awareness Effective

TV Anchor: Good morning, town of Gratefulness. Robert E. Tention here at Gratefulness Elementary School, where parents, teachers, students, and grandparents practice tai chi together three times a week as an intergenerational activity to combat ageism and memory loss. Principal Ortiz, please tell us how this program is helping the community at large.

Principal Ortiz: Good morning. Our community-based tai chi program is a health-education information delivery system that fits perfectly within our anti-ageism and memory-loss campaign. As an intergenerational activity, tai chi classes provide a unique social opportunity for children and older adults to share experiences. This helps dispel age-related stereotypes about themselves and others.

TV Anchor: Are there specific strategies for cost containment?

Principle Ortiz: Let me introduce you to our team of community volunteers and their functions.[4] For our community members who are fifty-five and older, Dr. B. Better will record baseline blood pressure before, during, and after each tai chi breathing and posture practice. For the young, school counselor Goodweather will be available to answer questions and cover ageism issues and memory-health topics prior to their participation in the sessions. The tai chi sessions themselves will be led by Randy Tai Chi.

TV Anchor: Counselor Goodweather, please share insights on how

---

4   "The Global Campaign to Combat Ageism Calls on Us to Act Together."

this intergenerational tai chi activity helps your teachers address ageism in the classroom.

Counselor Goodweather: Classroom teachers will learn how to breathe, settle down, and be aware of their own subtle forms of age bias. They'll think before acting on an assumption about a young student's age.[5]

TV Anchor: Are you referring to age bias impacting young people?

Principal Ortiz: Yes. For example, a classroom educator may have an unconscious bias in relating a child's age to an expected level of performance. But as Counselor Goodweather explained, slowing down to settle down, as in the tai chi postures, promotes the habit of with awareness of one's intention. As a result, there is a reduced chance of passing on negative age-based stereotyping to the next generation.

TV Anchor: And this approach ties into protecting the cognition and behavioral health of our children now before they reach retirement age.

Principal Ortiz: Children are our future.

---

[5] "Eradication of Ageism Requires Addressing the Enemy Within."

TV Anchor: Grandpa Frank, how has intergenerational tai chi practice benefited you?

Grandpa Frank: *Magandang Umaga.* As a young child growing up in Lyte, Philippines, I observed my parents and grandparents go through the aging process. It was terrible to hear them complain about aches and pains, sleepless nights, and loss of cognition. Over the years, I became depressed and unable to sleep, worried that one day I would share their fate. But while taking tai chi over the last twelve weeks, I learned how to breathe from my diaphragm to relax.[6] Now I can sleep peacefully throughout the night. Dr. B. Better says that sleeping better leads to a better memory. Along with better sleep, dividing the tai chi postures into short blocks of varied complexity also helps to improve my memory.[7] No more negative age self-stereotype for me, I am happy to report!

TV Anchor: So Grandpa Frank's early childhood experiences were fraught with age-related psychosocial stress that threatened his self-worth into his adult life. Dr. B. Better, the emotional impact is clear. What about the physical harm that tai chi can prevent as an intervention?

---

[6] "Proper Breathing Brings Better Health."

[7] "How Does Tai Chi for Memory Work?"

Dr. B. Better: Physical harm—yes! Stress hormones, which are helpful in the short term but damaging in the long term, can affect the immune system, leading to other health-related problems unless there is intervention.

TV Anchor: And what about you, Grandma Nancy? How has the socialization process, an important part of intergenerational tai chi classes, helped you?

Grandma Nancy: *Góðan dag.* I grew up in Ölfus, Iceland. My childhood experiences were not so different from Grandpa Frank's. But my parents and grandparents were physically and mentally active well up until their peaceful transition at age one hundred ten. At age sixty, my grandmother still skied. My granddad earned his shotokan karate black belt at age sixty-five and taught the art to children at the local youth centers. From observing them, I learned that getting old was just a social construct that did not apply to me.

TV Anchor: Wow! Your age-related stereotype is very positive. Then what is your need for intergenerational tai chi classes?

Grandma Nancy: It's not so much what it can do for me, but socializing with others in the class allows me to be of service to the young and people my age and older. And besides, I am a lifelong student with a lot more life left in me to enjoy.[8]

---

[8] "Ageism, Attitude and Health."

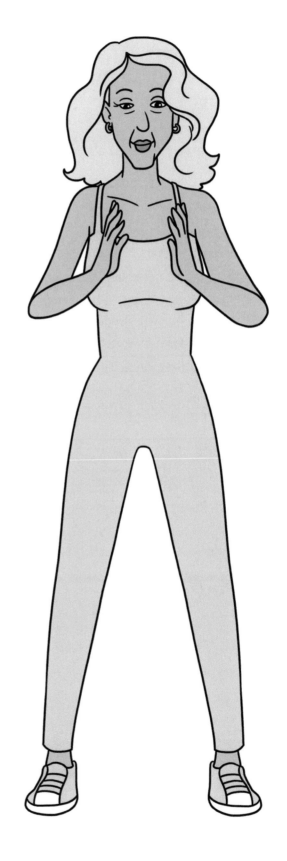

TV Anchor: Well, Grandma Nancy, you certainly look amazing for a woman your age.

Grandma Nancy: I think you should join our class. It will help you to avoid making such age-based stereotype remarks like that in the future.

TV Anchor: Oops! You are so right! My apologies.

Narrator: Both R. E. Tention and Grandma Nancy burst into laughter.

TV Anchor: Well, Randy Tai Chi, tell us—has intergenerational tai chi practice helped raise many of your classmates' awareness about ageism and memory health?

Randy Tai Chi: Yes sir, it has. Tai chi is a consciousness-raising experience.

TV Anchor: Can you provide an example?

Randy Tai Chi: Well, sir, have you seen that commercial in which an elderly person falls and cannot get up, but thanks to a device that person is wearing, she is saved?[9]

TV Anchor: Yes, I have seen it. Older people do fall.

Randy Tai Chi: Well, Mr. Tention, it's not only older people who fall; young people are subject to falling too. We asked our school counselor why the device was only targeted to the elderly. I think everyone should have one.

TV Anchor: Randy Tai Chi, your observation is on point; this is a clear indication that ageism has deep roots in our society. Our viewers would agree that Gratefulness Elementary School's ageism-awareness campaign and intergenerational tai chi are very important and very much in need.

---

[9] "Stereotypes of the Elderly in US Television Commercials from the 1950s to the 1990s."

Principal Ortiz: Mr. R. E. Tention, before you leave us, please join us as we go through our intergenerational tai chi postures one more time.

TV Anchor: I would love to follow along. And I invite our viewers to get up and follow along too!

Chapter 3: The Intergenerational Tai Chi Postures

1. Commencement

- (1a) Face twelve o'clock with heels touching and toes pointed to create a V shape.

- (1b) Turn your body to eleven o'clock.

- (1c) Lift your hands up to chest height.

- (1d) Lower your hands to your body.

- (1e) Place weight onto your right leg, and then step forward with your left-foot heel first.

- (1f) Position your right toe slightly behind your left foot, with your right heel up. Remember to breathe through each posture with slightly bent knees.

2. Lazy Tie Coat Posture

- (2a–2c) Rotate your arms clockwise from left to right. Notice that your arms circle around to chest height while you pivot on your left heel to conclude with right toe facing three o'clock.
- (2d–2e) Shift your weight to your right leg as your right hand pushes forward with fingers pointing up, followed by a half step with your left foot.

3. Open Hands Posture

- (3a) Turn your body to twelve o'clock by pivoting on your right heel.

- (3b) Bring your hands in front of your chest, fingers pointing up, toes pointing forward, and palms facing each other but apart to about the width your head.

- Breathe in and open your hands to shoulder width.
  Remember to breathe out when moving from 3a to 3b.

4. Closed Hands Posture

- (4a–4b) Breathe out and close your hands to the width of your head.

5. Single Whip to the Left Posture

- (5a–5b) With your left leg, step to nine o'clock and open your right arm to three o'clock and your left hand to nine o'clock. With your fingers pointing up, look at your left hand.
  Remember to inhale and then exhale when stepping to the left. Ensure that 70 percent of your weight is on your left leg.

6. Lifting Hands Posture

- (6a) Bring your right foot next to your left foot.

- (6b) Touch your right toe to the ground. Move your right hand down to your waist and your left hand above your head with your palm facing twelve o'clock.

7. White Crane Spreads Wings Posture

- (7a–7b) Move your right hand slightly above your head, with your palm facing twelve o'clock.

- (7c) Move your left hand down to chest level with your palms forward.

- (7d) Step forward with your right foot to push your hands forward, followed by a half step with your left foot.

8. Brush Knee and Twist Step Left Posture

- (8a) Turn to nine o'clock.

- (8b) Gaze at your right hand; step with your left heel to nine o'clock

- (8c-8f) Extend your right hand to push; follow up with a half step with your right foot.

9. Play the Pi Pa Posture

- (9a) Face nine o'clock. Step back you're your right foot, and extend your left arm forward to chest height.

- (9b) Shift your weight to your right leg; move your right hand to your body's center and near the left elbow.

10. Step, Parry, and Punch Posture

- (10a) Turn your left palm down and your right palm up.

- (10b) Step forward with your right foot as your right hand moves forward with palm down.

- (10c) Draw your left hand back to your waist with your left palm up.

- (10d) Step forward with your left leg, your palm facing forward at chest level.

- (10e) Punch forward with your right fist as your right forearm rests on top of your left arm.

11. Apparent Closed Posture

- (11a) Facing nine o'clock, bring your hands to chest level with palms facing forward.

- (11b) Step back with your right foot and bring your elbows to your body. Step back a half step with your left toe.
Remember to place 70 percent of your weight on the rear leg.

12. Carry Tiger to Mountain Posture

- (12a) Step forward with your left foot.

- (12b) Take a half step with your right foot.

- (12c) Face nine o'clock.

13. Brush Knee Right and Twist Step Posture

- (13a) Let your hands flow in a downward arc. Life your left hand up to shoulder height, palm up.

- (13b) Point your left fingers toward ten o'clock, turn clockwise to the right, and step out to the side with your right foot, with your toes pointing to three o'clock. Move your right hand to your waist and cross it over your left leg with your right palm facing down. Push forward with your left arm, palm facing out, toward three o'clock.

- (13c) Step with your left foot, bringing your left foot to the side of your right heel; look over your left hand.

14. Kick with Left and Kick with Right Posture

- (14a) Face nine o'clock, and lift up your left knee.

- (14b) Extend your left leg to kick with your toes; extend your left hand toward your left toes.

- (14c) Step down and turn your body that so that the right side is facing nine o'clock.

- (14d) Lift up your right knee.

- (14e) Extend your right leg to kick with your toes; extend right hand toward your right toes. Remember to inhale as you lift your leg and exhale as you extend your legs and arms.

15. Golden Rooster Stands on One Leg Posture

- (15a) Face three o'clock with your left foot forward and left hand extended at shoulder height. Hold your right hand palm down in front of your stomach, with 70 percent of your weight resting on your back leg.

- (15b) Step up on your left leg, and then simultaneously lift your right leg and right hand, with toes pointing forward.

- (15c) Advance toward three o'clock by stepping down with your right heel.

- (15d) Stand up on your right leg, and then simultaneously lift your left leg and left hand, with toes pointing forward.

16. Repulse the Monkey Posture

- (16a) Step back with your right leg, and bring your right hand to the right side of your head.

- (16b) Step back with your left leg, and bring your left hand to the left side of your head.

17. Closed Form Posture

- (17a) Face north.

- (17b–17c) Open and close your hands.

- (17d–17f) Extend your arms out and then down to your sides.

- (17g) Relax to allow your body and mind to settle down.

Chapter 4: Memory Is the Gift Seldom Forgotten

Grandpa Frank: I have a surprise for you, Grandma Nancy.

Grandma Nancy: Oh, Grandpa Frank! How lovely. My favorite flowers—the *Myosotis scorpioides*.

Randy Tai Chi: *Myosotis scorpioides*? I never heard of a flower with that name before, Grandma Nancy.

Grandma Nancy smiles: Well, Randy Tai Chi, these flowers are known to most as forget-me-nots. And they are just lovely! Thank you, Grandpa Frank. That was so thoughtful of you.

Narrator: Laughing together, the three continue on with their intergenerational tai chi practice.

The End!

Next time: Randy Tai Chi assists the military.

References

1. Andre, C. "Proper Breathing Brings Better Health." *Scientific American*, January 2019. http://scientificamerican. com/article/properbreathing-brings-better-health/.

2. Esposito, L. "Ageism, Attitude and Health." *U.S. News*, December 26, 2015.

3. Lam, P., et al. *How Does Tai Chi for Memory Work?* Tai Chi Productions, 2019.

4. Levy, B. "Eradication of Ageism Requires Addressing the Enemy Within." *Gerontologist* 41, no. 5 (October 2001).

5. Levy, B., et al., "Longevity Increased by Positive Self-Perception." Journal of Personality and Social Psychology 83, no. 2 (2002): 261–270.

6. Miller, D., et al. "Stereotypes of the Elderly in US Television Commercials from the 1950s to the 1990s." *Journal of Advertising History*, Special Issue, 2002.

7. "The Global Campaign to Combat Ageism Calls on Us to Act Together." *Nature Aging*, February 11, 2021.

8. "Ageism: A Social Determinant of Health That Has Come of Age." *Lancet*, March 18, 2021.

9. World Health Organization. *Campaigning to Tackle Ageism: Current Practices and Suggestions for Moving Forward.* October 23, 2020.